The Body Chaotic

The Body Chaotic

R.J. Pommarane

Sunfyre Books, LLC

First Printing: 2014

ISBN: 978-0-9903709-0-1

Sunfyre Books, LLC
PO Box 12024
Portland, OR 97212

Publisher Logo courtesy of: Copyright © 2014 by www.logoworks.com
Cover Art: Copyright © 2014 by Sunfyre Books, LLC
Author Website: www.rjpommarane.com

To my loving mother for always encouraging me to dream,
To Tara for being the best big sister possible, and
To Kevin for providing me with a rock to stand upon.

Contents

Part One: The Mind...................................... 1
Part Two: The Spirit................................. 16
Part Three: The Physical............................. 31
Part Four: The Sexual................................ 44

The Mind

Manic

He can't stop the thoughts streaming
Into his head, indecipherable moments
From the past, overwhelming his senses,
Driving him to the pits of insanity.

He talks and talks without breathing,
Going on about nothing as though
He were speaking as a prophet
Brining divine inspiration to

A world of petty heathens,
An unstoppable machine producing
Useless facts in a manner that drives
Others to flee from his presence.

His friends are tired and weary.
He rests alone in a sea
Of anarchy, wading towards the
Perpetual onset of psychosis.

Not seeming to care, he stands
There, his phone in one hand,
His dick in the other and his brain
Gone out the door.

The Body Chaotic

Carried away by the body chaotic
He stands in the inner workings of
His fragmented mind questioning
The validity of reality and wishing
For the wholeness and virtue of a
Real man. He is a broken man, an
Unexplainable anomaly destined to
Stand apart, to be distinguished not
By his successes but by his failings,
Doomed to wander in the shadow
Of a lightless world where the only
Consolation is the steady pulsing of
His heart, beating to the rhythm
Entrenched in his soul, the song of
A forgotten man struggling to attain
Sanity within a culture built upon
The perception that only the weak
Remain while the strong are always
Destroyed.

Psychotic Expressions

She sees nothing but
Vacant faces,
Staring with psychotic
Expressions of lifelessness.
Working hard to remember,
She finds nothing in the
Vaults of her memory,
Only wide empty space.
She speaks to the faces,
Asking how she came
To be in their presence.
There comes no
Answer to her questions.
Their mouths are
Etched from stone. They
Do not breathe, feel no breeze,
There is nobody home.
She braces her arms
Against her chest in fear of
The expressions on the
Faces. They look so real
But they are hollow and
Cannot feel.

Numb

Her mother pushed her hard to fulfill
Dreams readily imposed upon her,
Fantasies of success and fame never
Attained in her mother's youth.

She learned to play four instruments,
To speak French, Spanish, and Latin.
She spent her days reading Tolstoy,
Always her mother's favorite.

By the time she could drive they
Called her a genius and put her to
The test. They pushed her and pulled
Her in the name of success.

She couldn't take the pressure,
Began to secretly smoke and drink
Leading her dangerously to the
Solace of a dark syringe.

She forgot how to play their music,
She couldn't recall the words of other
Tongues. She stopped reading because
Of the headaches making her numb.

They found her in bed with a needle and
A note neatly held to her chest:
"Your prodigal daughter no more…"

Little Boy

There was once a little boy in pink trousers who
Would sit in his mother's garden and read. Each
Morning the other children would stop at the gate
And laugh at the boy all day. They called him a fat
Little faggot with a weak wrist and slow feet. The
Mean children made fun of his trousers, his pristine
And clean pants of passionate pink. They hated his
Trousers though he thought them smart. They threw
Rocks with weird faces, faces that told him he was
Less than them, a subservient form of waste meant
To live only at the convenience of others. The little
Boy grew aware of their hatred through a myriad of
Isolation and neglect. They would one day come
For him and drag him out into the night. They would
Tear him down and tie him up, leaving him to waste
Away in the damp green of a dark pasture. They
Will take his pink trousers and set them ablaze,
Forcing him to watch as his dreams are driven out
And replaced by the absence of love.

Crown of Roses

While wading in the pools of his thoughts
He spots an elusive badger burrowing away.

In the depths of his unconsciousness he
Comes to stand in a golden room where

Sits a throne of ivory. Upon the seat rests
A proud man that bears his likeness, but

Taller, stronger, and more alive. The man
Upon the chair stares down at him,

A gaze alight with celestial fire before taking
Up his crown of roses. *Now I know you,*

He thinks without utterance then awakens with
A growing warmth in his body, understanding

That nothing can harm him while he is
Protected by the king within.

Subhuman Fodder

Trauma apparatus of the mind,
Filtering diversity out of his
Monotonous life,
Closing off in self-imposed
Segregation while interpreting
Truth through antiquated doctrine,
Imposing martial law against
All who are called different,
Classified as the epignathic
Parasites of society.
Opposed to humanity,
All that are different
Facing the same fate:
Berated and sedated,
Mocked and abused as
Subhuman fodder from
The canons of fear.

Shining Star

Long absent from the modern world,
She doesn't remember how to act.
They tell her that she should carry
Herself gracefully and with poise,
To be quiet and modest and always
Submissive to the will of her man,
Particularly hard since she cannot
Recall her husband, having no
Memory of his face. She tried
With all her might to see a small

Memory, just a glimpse of the past,
Some miniscule remembrance to
Let her know she was in the right
Place, that she was actually living
Her life and not one made up by
The strangers in her face. But
Her mind remains empty, a
Hollow shell abandoned by the
Senses that dwelt within. She is
Forced to remake herself, to fashion

A new world in which she is the
Captain, steering her ships towards
A place in the stars where she may
Set herself to shine bright again.

Old Hermit

He never learned how to say I love you,
Was never warmed by the light of kindness.
He remains an unfeeling wretch called
Worthless by the voices inside.

His body remains numb as it
Ages without him. He remains
Forever twenty-one, trapped
In the tides of youth with no
Hope of escape.

He grows weak and feeble,
Unable to understand that
There are limited days for each
Man to live. Without love his
Days are left blank.

He will die alone, a naïve old hermit
That never learned the greatest lesson
The world can teach is to stand
Against convention and learn to
Love ourselves again.

Falsely Faithful Words

A frightened man
Screams as he
Destroys his body
In the name of God,
Fulfilling prophecies of
Ephemeral exorcism while
Pressing falsely faithful
Words against his heart,
Making love to the
Temptation of sin,
Tormenting his tortured
Mind with vices,
Waiting for the day
When he will be given
His final release.

R.J. Pommarane

Presence of the Present

He cannot be anything more than what he is,
A wandering minstrel from a bygone age,
Struggling to find his place in the sterile
World of modernity.

His values are obscure and his philosophy
Outdated. He is more a nobleman of the
Renaissance than a child of the
Generation of technology.

He finds it difficult to acknowledge the
Presence of the present. He wanders in the
Deep recesses of his mind, in a hidden realm of
Romantic chivalry.

The maze of unreality brings him to the
Edge of the cliffs of despair, staring out over
The fathomless abyss standing between him
And reality.

Suddenly, a white raven takes wing with
A wandering mage, soaring across the abyss
Landing gently on the widening island
Of the great beyond.

He follows the example of the raven,
Proudly returning to the world of the
Real to stand beside his peers and
Walk into the future.

Caulrophobia

Must flee from the place
Where they run rampant,
Laughing maniacally,
Glaring intently,
Moving hysterically.
He cannot get away
From the unreal within
The real, haunted by
Their smiles,
Living,
Breathing,
Eating,
Walking, running,
Talking, laughing.
He cannot see their
Beauty and for that he is
Ashamed.

The normal implodes
As he sees their faces
Everywhere.

Red Waves

He seeks for a way to be heard by
A world to which he means nothing. He fights
Daily depression to march onward towards his
Dream, but they don't care. They see only the
Marketable machinations of the mind, leaving
Everything else to rot away like a gangrenous
Arm blackened by a harsh winter snow. They
Tell him he will never be good enough, never
Fully personify the personage needed to
Succeed in the ravenous world of the real…

He fights the hollow feeling eating away at his
Soul, grinding down the desperate desires of
His wayfaring voice, leading him towards the
Road of temptation with every word they utter
In disdain. He feels broken. The roots of
His being are bleeding out onto the floor in
Red waves of convulsive terror, driving him to
The edge of madness, to ponder his choices,
To burn away the parts that send him into
The depths of dark depression…

Then, like the mighty phoenix, he will rise
From his own ashes and release upon the
World the undying radiance of his divinity…

Nightingale Pretenders

She is berated by the ones
That should love her,
Brought to her knees
By their corrupt and unkind
Nature. They spend their time
Drinking and fucking,
Scamming and stealing.
She reads and writes and
Goes to school, determined
To rise beyond her bonds
And make her body whole.
She tells her mother she
Wants to go to college. Her
Mother laughs, admits
She thinks nothing of her
Daughter. Still, she tries
With all her might to become
The woman she wants to be.
They laugh at her, mockingbirds,
Nightingale pretenders, attempting
To usher in the dusk and bring
Her dreams into their darkness.
But like ancient Icarus,
She builds wings from the
Hope inside her heart and
Soars away towards
The sun.

The Spirit

Hollow Echo

She throws the shutters open to greet
The warm summer rain, feeling the dull fire
Of mortality well up within her body.

The windows are open down to the depths,
To the twisted truth at the root of her bosom:
"The lights are off," she says with a vengeance,
"Nothing now remains but the
Hollow echo of a youthful memory."

The ashes settle on the shelf where her soul
Used to sit. The absence of the light makes
The room dark and blank. She finds it impossible
To predict what tomorrow holds for her
But she knows it will only bring sorrow.

She can feel the last of her strength escaping like
Air released from a vacuum so, without hesitation,
She slams the windows shut.

Pagan Dawn

The man speaks of matters meant to heal,
Words that can repair the hurts of the nations.

He talks of emotional fulfillment and acceptance
By the enunciation of his divine speech,

Truths spreading through the people as the
Waters of a flood spreading out from the sea.

But his words are suspiciously hollow, with meanings
Not always clear, calling the world with his

Irreverent charm, knowing the needs of the weak,
To whom he promises salvation. As millions

Seek his forgiveness, hunger and torture still exist.
The poor are still poor. The deaf cannot hear.

The dying still die and wars still rage in his name.
He says to stand with false prophets is

To be readily consigned to the flames of hell,
Unless we turn our will to his utterance

In repentance of our many supposed sins.
Yet a new day is dawning. Now

People see more than his flesh. They raise their
Voices eternally in words of defiance, screaming

As the man is forever consumed by
The light of the pagan dawn.

True Nature

Looking up at the sky,
Sometimes gray, mostly blue,
She heard a bird's wings
Flap, flap, flap, flap,
Creating gentle wind on
The unseen body of the air,
What a meteorologist describes
As the breath of the earth.
She saw it from the corner of her
Eye, soaring and reaffirming.

Who said the sky is blue
Did not know it as gray.
The bird flown away into death
Did not know its true nature.

Final Destination

He stares down the long dusty road
Stretching out towards his final destination.
There are no sidewalks, just rough
Gravel digging into his feet until they bleed.
He takes notice of the barren space
On both sides a lifeless desert of heat and
For a moment he believes he will
Sit down and die without reprieve.
Yet he gathers his strength and
Begins to walk the jagged little rocks,
Moving on down the dusty path
With his eyes fixed on the distant horizon.
Each step he takes make him age
But he knows he can never turn back.
Images begin to appear, visions
Of green vales and rivers of eternal bliss.

He smiles as he approaches the horizon,
Looking back a final time at the
Last days of his lonely life.

Gloaming

He called to his father
With a quiet voice

The same way
That a nightingale
Sings
& molts &
Sheds its body,

Flying away
To follow the eternal
Gloaming.

Breath of Life

The woman heard the lightning before it struck,
Cascading down from the heavens like
Water rolling down over giant boulders as
A place deep within her burrows into
The heart of all creation.

We are transmuted into earth when the
Day comes for us to lay down and die,
Relinquishing the breath of life as the stars
Shine in the heavens high above.
"Nothing lasts forever,"

The woman says from the shadows,
Knowing existence is perpetually fleeting.

From the Shadows

He writes in memoriam of the
Human spirits dwelling in the
Shadows, unable to break their
Bonds and see the truth of the
Reality in which they live.

The world has fallen into decay,
Marshaling in the time of the end
While mankind sits idly by, watching
As the oceans are poisoned and the
Land made barren.

The sleeper sits quietly within
His four walls, aching in his heart
Without reason, blind to the call
Within his soul urging him to live
As a steward of the earth,

Acting according to the
Divine principle that all
Living things walking
Beneath the sun are equal
In the eyes of God.

Immortal Reflection

She wonders if the mind is the extent of her being,
Tiny synaptic charges firing in the brain, granting
Her mobility and a means to focus her thoughts.
Is gray matter truly the place where she dwells?
Or, does she live deeper, in a place of shadows
Hidden from view by her own short sight.
She decides to go on a shamanic retreat to find
Answers to the question of life. They teach her to
Journey deep into the recesses of her subconscious
In search of a hidden stair. She descends the steps,
Leading her to a white hot room with no doors or
Windows. In the center of the room sits
A tiny orb of electrical energy, crackling with
The spark of creation. She walks towards
The object, looking longingly into its depths.
It is as though she is gazing into a mirror for it is
Herself that she sees. The her within the orb
Stands tall and proud, dressed in regal robes of
Sparkling silver with an emerald tiara for a crown.
There are no lines on the other her's face and she
Wears a gentle smile, looking back at
Her with knowing eyes, understanding all that
She yearns to discover. The moment she turns
Away it dawns on her. The she within the orb
Is the immortal reflection of her earthy soul.

Green Flames

He sprang from his mother
A wise old man wandering
The world in search of
Wisdom long since
Abandoned by the world
Of modern society.

He carries with him a staff
Of oak adorned with holly.
He twists into the hair of
His beard dried juniper
Twigs and wear a cloth of
Buckskin over his crotch.
He defies the men who say
He is crazy, a mad old
Hermit telling tales.
He dances naked in the
Woods around a fire of
Green flames, calling out
To dead gods for aid
Before returning gladly
To the warm womb
Of creation.

Colors of the Cosmos

She is a child of galactic awareness,
Born of the body chaotic, reaching
Towards the heart of creation with
The wings of a silver dove.

She paints herself with the colors of
The cosmos, affecting a hue that
Goes unseen as she turns back to
The world of the living.

She stalks the shadows in the dawn
And the dusk, watching and waiting
For a time when she can become
The goddess of tomorrow.

Waning Night

A woman stands on a cliff side,
Staring out towards the dawn.
In the distance, she sees a wolf
Walking beside a mighty angel.

The wolf howls while the angel
Takes flight, aiming for the blinking
Stars as a wormhole opens and
The world falls into silence.

She turns towards the waning night
Behind her, waiting until the end
When she too will spread her
Wings and visit paradise.

Lunch with God

He got a call the other day.
It was God inviting him to lunch.
They ate at a cart on the waterfront.

God had Tamales. He had Thai.
They sat together looking at
The river, eating in silence.

After their long meal together,
They walked on the promenade,
Speaking about the weather.

God did not preach and never
Mentioned faith. God let him do
The talking, listening intently.

By the time the sun began to
Fall, they had been walking for
Hours. He began to grow tired.

God reached out and took his
Hand, squeezing it gently while
He smiled with a teary eye.

"Are you ready?" asked God.
"I guess," he replied as God
Led him to the edge of the river.

Together they jumped, swept
Away by the currents, taken
From this life to the next.

Heavenly Mansion

The door closes as he wanders the halls
Beyond the world of the living, no longer
Bound to a single form, free to roam his
Heavenly mansion without fear of death.

The walls are painted the purest white
And the floors are hewn from marble.
Furniture sits spread throughout in a
Manner befitting a gentleman.

But as he wanders, he takes note that
There are no smiling faces, no warm
Embraces to greet him, no long dead
Former lovers to rekindle their flames.

His mother and father are not present,
His sister who died cannot be found.
He stands in the great expanse of
Those celestial chambers alone.

He tries to open the front door, to
Escape into the flowering fields beyond
But no matter how hard he pulls the
Door will not yield. He is trapped,

Destined to remain forever within
A prison beyond the stars.

Abstract Voices

He smokes ganja with Jah, his father,
Falling into the mirrored body before him,
Exposing the hidden nature living deep inside.
"I and I are speaking," he says, hearing
Two voices with quiet abstract voices
Whispering in the dark about life before
Returning to the world outside him,
Where his wife lies sleeping on the bed.

He wakes her with the voice of a wise man,
A prophet spreading words of peace:
"Em say da Rasta be watchin,
As da man be born ta rule
Seein em be in da soldier red
Preparin to overstand da truth."

The Physical

Foundations

She says:
My body is a temple.
He says:
Fuck that, have you
Seen this thing?

Pores are turning to plaster and
Organs are beginning to rust.
Windows are boarded over,
Measurements are imploding, and
Fixtures are burning to ash.
Tiles have come untethered and
The boards are warped and cracked.

My body is no fucking temple,
It's a building crumbling to dust.

Unholy Fire

Stretched out upon a dry salt flat,
He stares towards the sun,
Blinded by the yellow brilliance of
Its fiery visage. He knows that he
Will soon go blind. That he will
Never again see the wonders of the
World around him. His eyes
Fill with tears as he remembers
The bright blue hues of the calm
Tropical ocean and the pastel
Doors on the houses in Denmark.
He vividly recalls the face of his
Lover, the lines signaling the onset
Of his final years, the flecks of
White throughout his thinning hair.
He cries silently as he lays
There, the concert in full roar
Around him. The sun sets as
They light the wicker man afire.
As his eyes burn with the
Unholy curse of his affliction.
Suddenly, there is only
Nothing as his world descends
Forever into darkness.

Mockery

He was always perfect,
A mighty god walking with
Mortal men. His face was
Chiseled from white marble
By the hand of Michelangelo
Himself. But inside there lived
Something dark, haunting him
With waking dreams, a shadow
Settled deep in his spirit with
Selfish desires driving its will.

There in the darkness dwelt
A demon, a mockery of
A beautiful man.

Flesh Renewed

With a deep sadness she writes a recipe
To renew his flesh:

Dig the needle in a little deeper and
Let it pierce your heart, all the
Guilt should pour out as
If it were sludge escaping a
Cistern after a warm summer rain.
Wrap yourself in despair like
It was a warm and wooly blanket.
Try to see more than
The muddy contents of
A dirty syringe.

P.S. Repeat the process until
You learn to love yourself again.

Broken Body

A mother writes
To the son she lost too soon:

"I wish I had told you all the times you made me proud,
The days that you would show me you had become a man.
I wish you had known that you were very special
And never did me wrong."

"Other mothers had to endure sons who stole and struck
Them in anger. They would speak of their sons in
Sadness, describing their addictions to drugs
And unsafe anonymous sex."

"Then there was you. Sure…you were a bit lazy and your
Priorities were slightly askew but you never tried
To hurt me. More importantly you never dared
To bring hurt to yourself."

"The night the car accident took you from me I cried.
I buried my head in the blankets and, in the
Darkness wished to see your face again,
The man that I made."

"Your body was broken into pieces in the flames of
The wreckage and I couldn't see you again.
I just wanted to look at you a final time,
My one and only son."

Desire to Eat

The hunger tears him up inside,
His insatiable desire to eat.
He gained thirty pounds in one
Single week.

He hopes to start eating right
But lacks the fortitude to succeed.
He struggles to walk up the stairs and
Needs an inhaler to breathe.

His house is grimy and wreaks.
His cupboards are filled with
Cakes and sweets and his fridge with
Foods cooked in grease.

He sits in his chair because he
Can't fit in bed and sweats
In his own smelly warmth, lost
In a lime gelatin of remorse.

Lonely Addiction

She sits there watching him waste into nothing,
This vibrant youth she proudly calls her man.
"How did this happen?" she cries, unwilling to
Face her blindness towards his living joke.
He started in middle school with marijuana,
By the time he was sixteen, it was coke.
When he moved to the city he found meth to
Be cheaper and carried him further from hope.
He wasn't opposed to taking molly at a party
Or popping acid at an unending rave.
At first he said he could control it, that
The drugs were not calling the shots but like
All naïve children, he was living a delusion,
Permanently psychotic and broke.
Like an old man with dementia, everything
Slipped from his mind but his insatiable
Hunger to forget. It was a combination of
The meth, molly, and pills that brought him
Low that fateful day, when he collapsed in
Spite of his strength. They called her at work
With the terrible news and she flew to his side
Right away. Now she sits by his bedside watching
Him live by the will of a machine, knowing
That he will die just as he lived, lost in
The shadows of lonely addiction.

Temptations

As the moon settles high in the cold sky,
He stares at the place where his lover used to lay.
The mattress sags into a narrow dimple
Reminiscent of his partner's last horrifying days.
The pneumonia ate away at him slowly,
Making him thin and sickly and gaunt.
His lover didn't try to fight it, unable to
Stop the temptations of his flesh,
His chemical addictions fueled by a
Rebellious nature with a cynical effect.
He watched as his partner took to their bed
Unable to breathe without a machine.

On those last days, he prayed
But God did not listen. He had been
Forsaken, doomed to watch as his
Lover stood before the gates of heaven
To atone for his earthy sins.

False Youth

She thinks she has attained true beauty
In the likeness of desired perfection,
Buying tight dresses and exotic perfumes
To reinforce her false youth.

But others see her as she truly is, a
Tired sack of skin with yellow eyes
And rotting teeth, shriveled into a mockery,
An echo, absent humanity.

Without changing her bad habits,
She grows weak and spends her last
Days in bed. She no longer has the strength
To raise her weary head.

She dies the next day and they cry for
Their loved one taken too soon.
They beg God to be kind to her spirit and
Forgive her mortal sins,

Squandering her life in
A prison of forged from vanity.

Fragmented Minds

The long years of war did not
Strengthen his constitution or bring
Him peace of mind.
He thought he could conquer his
Cowardice by enlisting and going off
To fight the Viet Cong.

He returned to the States a different
Man, one scarred by tragedies he
Should never have seen,
Following mandates to murder
Innocent people in the name
Of liberty.

The terror boiled up at night
Invading the deeps of his dreams,
A prison of paranoia
From which he could never hope to
Escape. Everywhere he looked he saw
Their horrified faces.

He lost his wife and all his kids
From the hot, boiling anger of his
Fragmented mind.
He took to using Vodka to dull his
Senses but never forgot the deeds that
Led to his ruin.

He sat in his chair with his service
Revolver, thinking about all his memories.
He fired one shot, two, and then three,
Hitting the floor in a pool of blood.
He was finally free.

R.J. Pommarane

Quiet Desperation

He lost his power to speak from
An incurable disease of the larynx and
Became known as the hapless mute.
He writes with an eloquent speech no
Longer present in his absent tones.
Yet they continue to tease and abuse,
To taunt and discriminate, leading
Him to the epiphany that men would
Rather cast stones than try to understand
The quiet desperation of the hope
Lost along with his voice.

Champion of Hercules

He lies quietly in a hospital bed
Burning from the pain. Cancer, they
Call it, rare, incurable death of
The skin, quietly bringing him to
Realize the end of all things.
He remembers a time when his
Body was not broken and bruised,
A day when he was younger, the
Absolute specimen of male perfection.
Walking proudly above the common man.

He was the champion of Hercules,
An embodiment of divinity to lead
Lost men towards physical salvation,
Achieved through the admonition of
Earthly pleasure and the purging of sin.
He thought he would live forever, an
Ideal of absolute glory. That was
Before the doctors came to him
With the news of the disease running
Across his skin like the plague.

The sores on his body pulse with pain,
Writhing from the internal pressure.
They will burst soon,
Spreading their toxic venom like
A snake waiting to strike.
He is withered and weak, a shell
Long abandoned by the crab calling
It home, waiting to be washed
Away by the tides of death, ebbing
Slowly towards the stars.

He wonders what he
Will look like on the other side.

The Sexual

Miasma

She pulls him into her with the force
Of a lioness preying upon a young mate
As he opens the door to her inner desires,
Stretching her endurance to the threshold
Of pain, inducing a miasma of orgasms
That sweep across her body. She trembles
From the power of her primal response,
A perfunctory release of carnal pleasure.
She has no power of reasoning in those
Moments of sexual clarity. She knows
Only the overwhelming strength of his
Manhood driving hard into the heart
Of her being. She wants for nothing
More than to stay forever in his warm
Embrace, coiled into their tantric stance
Like ancient samurai bearing their swords
For the sake of their sensory honor. She
Wonders if she will ever feel more alive,
More in tune with the laws of nature.

She resigns herself to their release,
To the absence of their union, longing
For another morning of passion with
The man who haunts her dreams.

Quandary

Judging by the reaction in his loins,
He should be attracted to her,
But he can't feel the explosion of
Hormones in the pit of his stomach.

He is detached from his physicality,
Finding it impossible to understand
Even the slightest of details
About his sexual anatomy.

The quandary comes from the depths
Of his psyche, where there dwells an
Absence of comprehension and
The circuits are all broken.

There is no mending what he can't see
So he continues to live without desire,
Wanting nothing more than to be left
Alone with his own dysfunctions.

After work he rides the bus home,
Reading his book to keep his
Eyes from wandering and
Beginning the story again.

Otherworld Utterances

He falls through a rabbit hole each time
His lover touches his body with his lips.

He is taken to a world of exotic ecstasy
Where fish fly and birds burrow deep.

The joy of his earthly experience bringing
The divine to manifest in his hot flesh.

He reaches heaven and explodes in
Otherworld utterances of purity as

They drive their bodies together,
The universe makes perfect sense:

"There is no greater form of enlightenment
Than the communion of simpatico souls."

Carnality

She sells herself like a rare commodity to the highest bidder,
An auctioneer of human flesh, both the purveyor and the product.
"How much?" asks a man wearing an invisible mask as she
Stands on the corner in all her seductive glory.
She tells him the price then takes him back to her palace of
Swings, slings, whips, and various sex toys.
She twists his body in a machine of her own design until
He cries out in both pain and tormented pleasure.
"Shit," he screams, as she drives her commands deeper
Inside him, touching his soul with her lubed rubber scepter.
When she's finished she leaves him to bleed quietly on
The floor, returning to her royal court to await her next subject.
"Are you free?" asks another man as he approaches
The black queen of carnality.

Apollonian Wet Dream

He feels the winter wind washing over
His naked body as he thrusts his hips
Against the ground to release the
Root of his passion.
An erotic dream takes hold of
His mind as nude wrestlers take
Form, pinning him down with their
Manhood. He tries hard
To escape the visions but cannot
Exile the images alone, feeling his
Flesh in the bitter snow.
The spirits have numbed his mind
And brought his soul to a broken altar
Where he begs an unseen
God to heal his hurts and woes.
As he cries, God appears in a
Blaze of silver light.
He looks like an apollonian wet
Dream revived from the pages of
History within divinity.

The man shutters as he blows his
Load in the heart of ecstasy.

Pink Panties

He is a man, she is a woman, and
They share a single body. He wants
To fuck while she wants to feel
Emotions stirring within her.
He grunts and he farts, he snores
And he yells about little things
That annoy him. She speaks soft
Tones in elegant prose and always
Remembers her manners. He shaves his
Head and grows a beard while she paints
Her toenails red. He buys trousers but
She picks them tight and slips some
Pink panties in. He plays with his
Dick in the dead of the night when
She is deeply sleeping, dreaming of
Scarves, dresses of white, and a strong
Man to hold her.

He hears her pleas
For femininity
And
Curses the day
He turned out this way with
A woman living inside him.

Copulate through Compulsion

He never cared much for people,
Seeking out the company of others
Only to copulate through compulsion.
His bed partners were a diverse
Assortment of women, each with
Her own talents. He pressed in
Against their flesh like a carrion
Stalking its prey. He never once
Asked how the women felt when
It was over: He didn't much care.
He found it difficult to pretend his
Encounters meant anything more
Than sex. He refused to wear a
Condom for, even though he hated
Those who tried to tie him down,
He wanted them all to bear his
Children, to bring into being the
Continuation of his genetic line,
Bestowing upon the world
The burden of a new life.

Bi by Nature

She did what was expected and married young.
Her husband was tall and attractive with a kind
Face but he was not what she wanted. She was
Attracted to him enough, though she hated to
Touch him with her mouth. Her desire went far
Deeper than his callow flesh, from the feel of his
Troth inside her. She needed the erotic touch of
A woman. She dreamed of pressing herself against
The sweet mouth of an innocent youth blossomed
Into the fruits of femininity. She never told her
Husband that she longed for such things. She
Buried her secret deep, driving her desires to
The furthest recesses of her mind, never able
To erase the raw longings of her heart, denying
Being bi by nature.

Red-Eyed Monster

The red-eyed monster appeared
When they finished having sex.

He raised his hand and brought it
Down heavy upon her naked body,

Hitting her fast and hard until
He had expelled all his rage.

He called her a whore and spit
Fresh blood on her face,

Before driving his fist into
Her breasts again and again.

After he was sure she had
Heard him he sat and cried,

Allowing his guilt to wash away
His rage in angry heat.

He apologized before he dressed
And left money on the floor.

Driving home he washed away
The aches of shame before

Entering his house, going upstairs,
And kissing his wife in disgrace.

Kiss of Death

Even after the doctor told him the news,
He refused to wear condoms. He told
Himself he could not give it to another
Man, that he was somehow above the
Basic laws of biology. Convinced of his
Sexual immunity, at least in the vile
Propagation of the disease, he went
Back to the baths and the P&P's. He
Laid down beside men young and old
And brought them under his sway,
Coupling in sweaty passions until he
Had found his release. In the month
That followed his visit to the doctor he
Slept with more than fifty men, denying
Every day that he was bringing harm to
Them. For three more years his life was
The same, his goals completely unchanging,
Until he found himself in the presence of
A man with whom he had once been.
This man who was once vibrant
Was wasted and overly thin, marked across
His flesh by the black sores of cancerous
Defeat. He expressed his sympathy to
The dying man, who simply spit in his face.

He had become a murderer in his denial,
Spreading the kiss of death.

Ambiguity

To him ambiguity is not appealing to
A world that values black and white.
He cannot be a woman if he bears the
Mark of manhood, adorning his hairy
Chest and wrinkled brow. He is tall
For his demographic with a wiry voice,
Deep and raspy from the consumption
Of cigarettes.

Yet there yells within him the elegant
Voice of a lady, calling out to be
Recognized, to seek the insatiable
Gratification of her androgyny.

Skin Deep

Falling into love with his flawless body,
Not seeing the devious nature shining
Menacingly from within his eyes. He is
Not a man to be trifled with for his sex
Is his greatest weapon, stronger than
The tip of an arrow or the back of an
Angry hand. A delinquent master of
Manipulation, his only concern is the
Completion of his own conceited and
Arbitrary ambitions in the face of an
Authority greater than man. Each one
Of his conquests, each time he rubs
His sweaty flesh against another naked
Body, he sees it only as a victory, a
Confirmation of his carnal conquests.
His only mission is to discover the
Perfect rhythm through which he
Can subjugate other men with the
Vain and sinister will of his only desire.

His sexual forays are too many
To count and, with each passing release
Of pleasure he sells more of himself to
The demons of lust, in exchange for
Perfection that is only skin deep.

R.J. Pommarane is proud to have been born and raised in Oregon, discovering the wondrous Mysteries of nature at an early age by exploring the woods with his father's family. R.J. graduated from Portland State University in 2008 with a BA in English before going on to attain an M.A. in Education in 2011. Since then, he has devoted his time to the contemplation of his own resolute spirituality, particularly through the expression of the written word. Both a poet and an author of fiction, R.J. currently resides in Portland, OR, with his life-partner and two cats.